TEMPLE SONNETS

nathan smith

COPYRIGHT © 2005

WITHDRAWN

AN EARTHBOUND BOOK

PUBLISHED IN THE BERKSHIRES, MASSACHUSETTS

ISBN # 0-9771818-1-2

An EarthBound Book
Published in The Berkshires, Massachusetts
Printed by The Studley Press, Dalton, Massachusetts

For Mari

Temple Sonnets: SPRING

Temple Sonnets: SUMMER

Temple Sonnets: FALL

Temple Sonnets: WINTER

SPRING

EQUINOX

TS191

Meta Forces coalesce into
   a Universe speckled with galaxies...
      brighter because the space is blackened so —
   instinctively the wide attention flies
with swift intent towards one, traveling through
   its constellations, seeking a solar system
      spinning at its galactic rim — as though
   it were a beacon, but tiny as an atom —
there a marbled sphere comes into view...
   a planetary fleck bathed by a star
      one half aglow the other half in shadow
   while around it storm clouds swirl and whir
and standing on a parcel of this blue
   green planet, I encounter Spring today

TS461

at the freezing's aftermath when the burgeoning sun
  calligraphies the shadows of the budded
trees in wavy verticals upon
  the waning white strata of Winter, headed

in a convoluted torrent on
  a journey through the grey geography
whose possibilities have re-begun
  like a resumed discussion on some philosophy

seducing my Consciousness into the green
  unraveling of Spring that stuffs my sight
with so much seeing that my being can
  completely incarnate into the thought

of it... so I arrive where I began
but enlarged as the spiral the hawk spins over the land

TS462

on a dark hill lately winter haunted
the searchlight sun showed a circle of trees
with branches bare except for probabilities —
a studied look revealed that color had sprouted
faintly, proving (if anyone could care)
that life indeed was really living there
the Winter's passing was not to be disputed
even though the sunshine show was brief
it's hard to keep a negative belief
when word is out a ray of hope was spotted
despite one's thoughts have hardened into stone
the heart wants sky and flails in its cage of bone
I myself sometimes have even sprouted
visions that at other times I've doubted

TS479

a brush pile in a pasture, tall as a small
house, was razed to earth one April morning
smoldering grimly from its recent burning
I came across it after its fiery thrall:
reduced to char and shallow as a puddle...
a hump of embers glowering in the middle
with singed and wilted things around it all

I could have imagined the site as a city embattled:
a towering thing ... its torching... an empire toppled
that no amount of trickery could forestall
a moment more   calamity had come
though not upon the tyrant's house this time
but rather on the mice, as I recall,
who nested in the wood pile since the Fall

TS1

in a night filled with thrashings, fears and sighs
   something, someone called me from my sleep
   wake up! it said *the dark is full of hope*
draw away the curtains   *in the sky's*
   cosmology I've put an opal moon
   to prove to you that you are not alone
surrender to your waking   *now*   *arise!*
   I rose and witnessed through the window
   the moon's translucent opulence on meadow
tree... all breathing things and otherwise
   then I gathered up my forces, went outside
   to stand among them when the Presence said
be still   *be light-full*   *open up your eyes*
remember you are One in paradise

like little grey mice from the muddy mind of earth
the pussy willows come — the passionate death
   of the Winter giant coaxes them to peak
in to the indecisive atmosphere
(today a freeze tomorrow maybe fire)
   if night is warm enough the peepers croak
their sweet falsetto code, assuring me
that I've traversed the incubating time
   again... and if I choose to I can speak
about the prophecy of April's reign
its golden age of daffodils and benign
   indifference to snow, its verdant cloak
and vernal flowers declaring all the while
renewal is the sole enduring rule

TS468

after the long stillness the trees moved —
the visible sign of the invisible presence trifled
with the birds, clattered the branches, disheveled
    the clouds and caused me to question what I perceived

the lilac leaves, appearing on the scaffold
    of the lilac bush, were premonating lilacs —
    grass was sprouting out like cowlicks
on the heads of hills while downwards rolled

    the rain in trebled rivulets — lakes
engorged — trickles became torrents — the world
had plunged itself into desire and would
    have nothing of its former looks

or wintry clothes, but rather be beheld
    like a serpent of wind reinventing itself as it goes

TS4

Spring breezed in — the air was in flower
flowing with intention   like a river
full of coursing through the sprouted landscape —
Winter seemed so far away... as if
it were as insubstantial as a whiff...
such is the dexterous mind   when Spring takes shape
you'd swear a stuffy room had had its windows thrown
and inhaled outside to its very bone —
now was the beginning of all of Winter's hope
as it has been for vast millenniums
when color and perfume unfurl from stems
familiar as Winter gurgling down a slope
this sense of scented-things, so immense
that the past is blossomed in the present tense

TS196

all that killing that the steely mind
of Winter brought to wood and meadow makes
me wonder what's the use of all the dying
since the ground will rise up green, the spread
of sun will put the white and purple in
the lilac, the beech will reinvent its leaf
and sluggish snake will leave its narrow burrow

the Future convinces the farmer to seed his furrow
like a fallow mind will with a fresh belief
for down in the marsh the muskrat wakes the skin
of the glistening water while the doves thread
through the aromatic morning crying
Winter returns whatever it takes
Spring, though buried in Time, is what I'll find

TS3

from their underworld routes, the mortal
trees conceive an abracadabra of buds
and in an ecstasy they flood the woods
now the razing and rising the natal and fatal
moment confirmed by amphibians swelling the swamp
where feathered creatures call from bough and stump
thickening the air with sound as the petal
thickens the sight and smell — and add to these
the green vocabulary of the leaves:
a language of an elemental people
conversing in layers and layers of whispers... yet
I feel that I can make some sense of it:
they're saying:, *welcome, your presence is Essential*
and remember: you are walking in a temple

TS311

in this protracted moment of the year
when the buds begin to yawn and creaky trees
commence to stretch their limbs and send out leaves

like scouts investigating the Spring frontier

groundhog raccoon opossum skunk and mole

separate things manifest from the hole
for the experience of vernal air

restless with confinement in their hidden
burrows and emboldened by the sudden
sound of the wind and water worlds roar-
ing overhead — the sky pulls back its drapes
and like a thaw the light pours down the slopes
and soaks the valley's green emerging floor
illuminating all the life it shapes

the cleft earth, the seed's strightened shaft
  the excited peepers peeping and I admit
that this is the albino season's gift
to me; who revels in its petal drift —

  when Winter deepened, I was upset
  because the tepid yellow sun could not
provide an ordinary indoor plant
  a windowsill with one warm spot

but fret proved unproductive so I spent
  those last snow-dying days becoming full
as night is with the moon's environment
Now is the moment like striking stone to flint

  the vegetation blazes, the moon's a ball
  of platinum fire and I burn with them all

TS308

the far foreseeing mind can recognize
that Spring is destined to be blossom wise
   experience and memory have proved
that   in the Autumn when the shaggy skies

   were loud with going geese, the geese conceived
   of coming back – since then the Winter has heaved
and hammered hard…setting the branches gnash-
   ing from an egocentric wind which shoved

itself through any opened space it wish-
ed… although at times the woods were still as ash-
   es after fire   like a mind at last
at peace with its own burning   the volatile hush

   again evolving to a full blown forest
   with wintry-thoughts as far away as east from west

TS313

the paradox of sunset at its zenith
and an indigo evening bringing the planet Venus
up like sea glass scuttled upon a strand:
day and night caught in an act of genius

the in-between time where I can stand
like silent-space parenthesized by sound
that middle place of power of pure potential
like the soul ascending out of its burial mound

consider even now the contrapuntal
patterns that the peepers make... essential
as April where they gather to sing together
with whatever else is stirring on the mantle

of earth whose ferns are unfolding their emerald feathers

a temporal moment suspended between two forevers

TS465

wasn't it only a moment ago the ground
began contracting like a stone
and a raw north wind with a needling rain
determined to put a chill into my bone

and the pewter sky collapsed on all below —
but I have seen some browsing robins though
and other birds with skimming beaks respond
to ripplings on the surface of the pond

the signs say: *Now, what's old is re-begun*
or differently put: *Now, something's done*
(my point of view determines what I know)
it's almost as if someone waved a wand...

the subcutaneous earth sucked in the snow
and out of gratitude conceived the frond

TS2

Time has come full circle in its passion:
Consciousness is coming out of clay
green and guileless as a girl and boy
   discovering their sexual equation

not since last year's tender ground swell
when the frieze of trees against the hill was full
   of rainy wind and antler-like percussion
was there such an understated ready-
ness to make the world's berth so rowdy

   a 'giving way' and 'taking over' tension
seduces everything unseen and seen

like the gravity and lightness from the moon

   I am affected by its cyclic mission

with resurrected passion young and green

TS211

I hoped with all my hope to hear the shrill
    meow the catbird cries — I hoped to watch
    the crocus, like a mitt, spread out to catch
a grey sky rumbling through the valley, spill-
    ing warm beneficence and wind across
    the meadow's fresh society of grass
flourishing with bees... when failing Fall
    convinced the birch's juices to withdraw
    into the root and make the branches bow
in deference to a whiter weightier will —
    but Hope is a path to take me where I want...
    like here: a place of contrasts where the slant
of mid-day mid-May sun is not at all
    concerned with how the frostbit flowers did

TS485

Time and Intent conspired an afternoon
   like this that weathered the Winter's gigantic force...
inevitable as the eye drawn towards the moon
   predictable as when the snows immerse

themselves into their watery psychology —
   the leaves are lucent membranes full of flutters
   not yet versed in dusty Summer matters
or waxing Autumn's cold cosmology

Now is the moment after the peepers croon
   before the air burns blue and plants turn leggy
when the tangled woods become a flickering screen
   to camouflage the animal biology

coming to nurse at the unconditional stream
   swirling through their burgeoning universe

TS209

I knew that this would happen: the hero
and heroine were bound to make it to
the seasoned world's Spring scenario:
where Winter, with its white and zero
weather, decreases like an echo

Now is the dream they had planted long ago

the sky evolving to a visual crescendo
the dark horizon glowing with a halo

every pulse and impulse with its psycho-
sensual death and birthing innuendo

the unfurling grief and triumph of Triumph too

the microcosm mirroring the macro

what else can a man and woman do?

I can't discern a difference between the two

TS14

on Heavenly-Earth the morning bleeds like ice
   into the after noon   as smooth as dying
paratrooping thistles make a grace-
   full exit   eloquent as improvising

      sunrise on a mountain's body   crickets
in a fiddling frenzy offer paradise
      their resumes   from green sequestered pockets
the rabbit scoots   with courage   becoming wise

   my eye evaporates itself in seeing
the flash flood weeds in flower   every place
   through day and on the other side of evening
insects add their auditory spice

      heralding the future like the prophets —

      the deer, I hear, are nesting in the thickets

TS336

in the spiral of Time with its swirling undertow
the meadow has had a run-in with the plow
and fenced in spaces catch the calf and colt
who know no other than what men allow

the mind and artifact are worked with gilt
shaking the eye like an ear by a thunderbolt
while whistles stab the quiet of the river
lying on a bed of barren silt

ferns in a furious chain reaction quiver
where an elusive species flees for cover
demolishing the spider's lucent net
uncoiling the black snake from its lover

on the one hand I am unsure how I fit
and on the other hand I can't forget

TS475

imagine a fingernail moon with a smear of clouds
across its blade-like edge to wipe it clean —
then dawn… and a row of vertebrae-like beads
along the arching backs of ubiquitous green

gold grasses — boldly, as fast as weeds
flowers foliate the fields that lately speared
the Spring early earth   while the enlightened woods
make leaves persistent as an unchecked beard

branches and canes prepare for their succulent loads
where lately the cold galloped over the country side
in indiscriminate haste, heading towards
an interview with all it once defied

yet the rose surrounds her velvet self with swords
even while the warm wind ranges wide

TS471

grim clouds slouched over the uneven
west   while the firs had a worried waving to them
the seamless world of air passed through them

it seemed like weather conjured by a coven
hidden in claustrophobic woods

the wind pushed through the maple neighborhoods
evicting their leaves and inviting the starkness in...
pushing them like a dog would push the deer...
but where it meant to push them wasn't clear

birds scattered after a safer haven

for ominous forces were fitfully starting to merge
and, in their exponential manner, surge
across the habitat... limbically driven
like mice conspiring to get the cat

TS13

like a cloud I wrung myself, squeezing as much
　　of me as possible into my task
(it wore me out to work at such a pitch
but I thought that was how one birthed a wish)

　　at any rate there was no going back
I'd set my will in motion... done the deed...
　　like planting seeds with just a pointed stick
　　with no assurance there'd be fruit to pick

but better that my heart was bled
　　and faint from doing what I loved to do
than bleeding over something that was dead
because there was no love in what I did

　　yet even as I justified that to
　　myself I said, *I cherish what you do*

TS23

like the River of Time, a wind rolled over my window
sill last evening, bringing memories
of where it visited — olfactory stories
that the woodchuck, poking from his burrow,

sniffed with interest to assuage his worries —
smelling the dispensation of rain, its arrow
drops fussing the dust and feeding the willow
and the pollen falling fast in yellow flurries

while thunder jangled and clanged the quiet hollow
puddles of bluets with petals like butterflies
consigned their essences to the mysteries
of night like the tunneling mole below and the narrow

reptile's rendezvous with one who dies
and the farmer's wonder over his planted furrow

TS337

time climbs towards the solstice event

   cricket riffs waft over the meadow
   which only hint at what's about to follow

maneuvering underworld-things invent
   concentric circles on the liquid surface
   confirming the presence of other universes

galaxies of Mayflies cause an incident
   in the lower levels of the bird-lively sky

   as the meadow's face aspires to my thigh

the chlorophyll-spear is constantly making its point

   the season is pregnant with such a hunger that
   the chipmunk's been beheaded by the cat

while the hyacinths and peonies anoint
   the garden world with its tyrannies

TS343

with every Spring's return I re-remember
how the Cottonwoods flurry like December —
   it's worth the circumnavigation of
the year to harbor in the month of June...
with never a better celebration scene —
   with every windy whiff a blizzard of puff-
s are off and free like helium balloons
filling this fateful eve with miniature moons
   that skate around the house and over the roof
then cluster together like frog eggs in a shallow
though softer than you'd guess an angel's pillow —
   I can imagine a boulder to be a cliff
and the feathery seeds the sea foam at its feet
and I a sailor relieved at a site so sweet

SUMMER

SOLSTICE

TS509

it's about a way of seeing things...thought lost —
told in legends, embellished over the ages —
known equally to idiots and sages —
carried over continents and vast
uncharted oceans — it was, although beset,
unstoppable as water through a net —
North and South from Center, East and West
it spread like birdsong and rushing waters...
was told by parents to their sons and daughters
in every culture, race and creed and cast
inexorable as the spinning of our planet
far reaching as the journey of a comet
appearing everywhere... like common dust —
the tale of shaking hands... not the fist

TS66

consider Time (if Time were linear)

imagine long ago… before these woods
were anything but woods and ley line roads
    connected being here to being far

crickets cricketing sing from the weeds

    the catbird's strange meow is in the leaves

    the coo and whistling wings of mourning doves
cause man and woman to up-turn their heads

    the screechy sighs the hawk makes come in waves

crows call to their mates to come and sample
a feast down in the hollow where the bumble-
    bees abide with flower-life and us

consider this (I have)… we're wisely simple
standing at the threshold of our Temple

once, when the world was young and wondrous to see
   …fern-like, I unfurled in green degrees —
   like lakes, my eyes reflected back the skies
and day was an epic poem surrounding me

   and like a bird, I noted, with cyclic surprise,
the closing dusk, the coming dawn — and far
away was closer than the speed of fur
   for food or faster than the feather flies

Enlightenment was what I came here for
   the luminous reach of the moon among the woods
   the ritual-flowers crowning the heads of the weeds
where real and imagined are each other's metaphor

   green, the gardens grew… speckled with beads
that morning dropped… and dropped this morning too

the morning, in a full euphoric swing,
   had flowers poking from the lanky green
   meadow… mowed by me on my machine —
out in front of its mechanical whirr and clang
   (not only threatening to do some harm
   but at the same time sounding an alarm)
something in a furious hurry flung
   its slender self across my line of vision —
   it took a micro-moment for my reason
to fathom, *what exactly was that?* hurling
   off into the storm of swirling grass…
   I waited a moment more to let it save its ass —
I'll bet, if there are angel-frogs some sang…
if not, I'll bet, at least the Bluebells rang

TS37

on the mirror of the pond a salamander
hovers… half below and half above…
its little lungs in love with the unseen air —
the sun's in overflow and warmer than a glove

out from the murky underneath a stand
of inquisitive reeds pokes through to take the view —
then, with a secretive sound, the dextrous wind
divides them, bending their slender bodies too

fish adroitly fish the lapis cave
of sky… then into murky depths descend —
the muskrat slices the water and a wake and a wave
arise… then magically the waters mend

like the grasses that gather to cover over a grave
or two beliefs I thought would never blend

TS377

there — with the muttering hum of honeybees
there, where I have to get down on my knees
    I get the chance I normally would not:
to see the way the sphinx-like spider sees —

    thither and yon her cables spread tightrope taut
    forming a scaffold over the perennial plot —
languidly, as unhurried time, she stretches…
    and yet, she's ready as a desirous thought

she's clever as ever at keeping the grasses in stitches
and, at such flowery altitudes, she catches
    things of many ilks and different sizes —
she must be from the clan of the weaving witches

    casting her web like a spell on the garden, which seizes
    the stinging things in their gentle enterprises

TS231

a quiver of feathers litters the orchard floor
the legless reptile underneath the bush
   lies belly-up — the scaffold of a deer
bleaches in a heap in the after-hush

   of pain and maggots — two gaping sockets
tunnel to an emptied skull — at the door
   outside the wolfish spider's den the cricket's
crisp carcass hangs by a hair

   lilies, sprouted early on like rockets
give a withered look to lookers-on
   while the mouse floats bloated by the bucket's
brim my insensible mind, like a falling stone,

   plunges its self into this death wish
world, when the under becomes the overtone

TS61

when Consciousness drops its corporeal glove
   when its sloughed off molecular-self is dispersed
as ice is in an April pond... still the shove
   of the punctual sea to shore will be reversed

   and the bee will still store honey in its hive
the thunderhead, like some huge broiling fist,
   will curl out its brooding self and drive
the drought away — dusk will still be fished

for insect food by nervous bats, and the red
   of day's exhaustion still will blaze the eye —
cosmic messages will still be read
   in those whose destiny it is to die

   like the dotted fawn turning to the doting doe
   whose tracks are temporary as the snow

TS27

the dark cross of the vultures, stirring the blue
caldron air say... something simmers in
the dregs with fungus, root, sloughed-off skin
and other leaving things whose time is due

the mole is making an undermining din
below the rose, like a papal fire at
the feet of some dark Beauty that
was lusted for for merely having been

the meadow mouse, who once escaped the cat,
courageously comes back...as in a thriller
though, the trap is slyly set to kill her

darknesses of every kind infat-
uate the heart and mind   I want to tell her
today   I heard a cricket in the cellar

TS58

in a day advanced to middle age, in a darkling
wood, sensitive to breezes, a swatch
of sun lit up a limb like frozen lightning
and instantly, like one great emerald match,
the vivid leaves were struck and glossed with gold

nothing about me could keep me from lifting my face

a messenger was entering my field
of vision from some undetected place

and then my eye beheld the feathery reach
and smooth articulation of the flying
thing: its flap and glide and hover and perch

we watched unthreatened and unthreatening:
two beings: hawk and human flesh who hold
significance in the texture of Paradise

TS82

in a meadow under rain a ruddy buck
  (whose antlers make a bony symmetry
above the thirsty goldenrod) comes back —
the slick drops with their tick, tap and click

  make hissing sounds like a fire sizzling softly
the buck, browsing the meadow, in the incident
  of rain on trees in their temporal pageantry
  turn time into lyrical poetry

though morning is old, day is not nearly spent
  so who can say how long this rain will last
or his maneuvering through this delicious environment
yet all there is is now   in any event

  colossal forces converge providing the grist
that makes this moment matter to the quick

TS59

a meadow makes an oval in the wood
where galaxies of Queen Ann's lace gleam
in the green-black space beneath the snowball moon
while willows bending over a silver hoop
of water wade in moss as stunning as green
glass with morning pouring through it   a pool
of coolness instigates the spirity mood
of mist   where frogs converse in cluck and cheep
among the knuckly roots   mushrooms bead
like blood drops   beside an eddying creek
day withdraws like shutting the door
to the room of a cradled child who's off to dream
of ways there are to enter human-hood
where life is to be lived not understood

TS38

the curved horizon always up ahead
 the hawk hatched from an egg, too tight
  the nature of pain and expectation of Beauty
   the raptor cruising the bright abundant air
    the sibyl clouds prophesying rain
     the beauty of Nature and pain of expectation
      the invitation from the web to enter
       the stringed mandala and spider at its center
      the nature of pain and beauty of expectation
     the rioting colors coming to seed again
    the blackness embracing the firefly's flare
   the expectation of pain and nature of Beauty
  the ubiquitous ambiguity of night
 the platinum moon in its inward turning mood

TS215

the sky became a gray balloon that burst
like a simple mind that held too large a thought
no matter how it held it simply wouldn't fit
and what it was before it was now not...

I watched while, with a swift translucent stain,
it put a gloss back on the Summer's green
obsession, thirsty from the humid noon-
s that had been strung together in a chain

rain is something you really don't forget
when you have not had near enough of it

unsated desire nags like an ache at the brain
fulfillment and relief can't come too soon

like when it seems the rain will never quit

and all you want is sun to flood the room

the woods don the idea of nocturnal time
quicker darkened than the field, whose face
is opened like an eye to catch the close
    of daylight   bit by bit the earthy home
of beast and bird moves towards its unseen end
as the silky collision of leaves with leaves sound
    applause for such a day's finale, whose prime
intent is to bring opposites together —
ever onward, for forever, further
    westward, where the world has an eastern name
the masque of time bequeaths this twilit scene
to yesterday, today, to everyone…
    tomorrow too… this re-occurring theme...
constant and steady as breathing or blood pulsing through

TS55

magic? where? an August evening wind
   unfurls a lullaby in an uneven voice…
yet sweet as any whistling bird around —
   crickets in soft decibels advise

the memory to store them for the Winter —
   dragonflies draw unexpected patterns
over the simmering meadow, achieving a fainter
   version of itself, as evening turns

its marbled sky to coal and cools the land —
   owl-quiet, night erases matter
like a body erased from its dreaming mind —
   fireflies from out of nowhere enter

   making points and dashes of light with their lanterns
a coded message the insight gets in flashes

TS359

dusk already tipped in favor of
day's darker enterprise — off
flew the birds to their roosting altitudes
whistling one last melodious riff

night flowed in ...with the precision ...of the tides
the light ebbed out as the stars came in as guides —
later, under clouds coyotes hunted steep
woods and shushing grasses waving in glades —

my eyes startled open — even in my sleep
I heard them — their yelping boiling up
through the muggy mountains the blackest shade of green
then all of a sudden... silence   like a sprung trap

the woods were filled with light as if the moon
exploded on them like a burst balloon

TS60

picture this: a whole moon hoisted half
way up the pacifistic sky, the hum-
ming bird's hum in the evening's equilibrium
the breeze's variation on itself
to make the treetops seem as if they swim
and above it all the Milky Way is splashed
like luminescent pollen through the hushed
eternity of space, whose darkening plum
complexion is the color I fervently wished
for… when the sky was a sea of sunshine and
it seemed its august heat would have no end

now picture this: the eastern air is washed
with the consciousness of a resurrected kind
because that's what the vision wants to find

TS232

Time is the home of the Black-Eyed Susan
whose face is wide like amazement, as the solar
   part of day becomes the evening season —
   Time puts pastels in the Rose of Sharon
and seduces the bumblebee to briefly anchor
in a bee balm   like a treasure hunting sailor
   the moth that mimes the hummingbird
dips in to sip it's deep rouge color —
   Veronica spreads its indigo by the yard
     while Phlox convene in a white and purple hoard
(the flower's the thing to which the seed is driven)
   'til time, as always, raises up its sword
and beheads them all... because death is a given
as certain as the dazzling red horizon.

the fact of the matter is: the last round moon
of Summer softened midnight with its milky
glaze — after that the tardy rain
came teasingly to clean the trees and stocky
rocks, the blood-red beauty of ivy along the road
is sparking off a general conflagration —
the reed becomes a phallus full of seed
that wishes its lover-wind to be its ruin
the oak has lodged itself into the mood
of acorns in a world growing spare
preparing for the huge white flood...
informing me of all of this and more:
the first-come daffodil has long been dead
as it has died so many times before

overturned...the field, freckled with crows
   coming together to dine, picking its bones —
   the upturned worm, compliments of the tines —
the limp length of the snake loops from claws
   that shuttle it somewhere up into a nest
   whose greedy fledglings anticipate a feast —
with its albino hair the thistle snows
   into the realm of possibility
   like thought creating its reality
the temperature of falling Summer flows
   into a chill where my once invisible breath
   exposes itself to the world of wings and teeth
over and over   again   the impulse grows:
   the cat so loves the bird she eats his death

TS88

one more evening being lightning-torn
with slanted silver slivers raining —
one more mellifluous wind's return
with scents and sunrise re-creating morning —
vines unwinding and blossoms being born
as periscoping bulbs break ground,
while sampling what the worms are churn-
ing underneath the green hair of the mound —
Idyll Time in a marriage of fruit and thorn
and one more upstart thrush to mark its waning
and the world evolving... taking another turn
and none can change it even as it's changing
and change is the cutting and closing of the wound
and no amount of time brings on its taming

TS86

the blue-eyed sky opens its cloudy lid
　to contemplate the withering and brown
　inflection coming over leaf and lawn —
crocus, lilac and lily have long been abed —
　the vernal earth is verging on the dawn
of undoing the vegetation that it did —
a milkweed opens like a launching pad
　stuffing the afternoon with flower down
though many a bloom has yet to come to bud
　soon enough my window will have grown
　the fern-like frost that only cold can spawn —
then the white deluge from overhead —
　but like a fish in water will not drown
Time and its turbulent element are wed

TS237

I've considered how September had
   to shed the sheath of August to become
   September (any season I could name
is only what it is because it shed
   itself of what it was) who can doubt
   that Fall arrives by merely sliding out
of Summer as gold does out of goldenrod
   or puberty emerges from the child —
   the future is a vision to behold
   projected outward from the present, driven
   to perfect the perfectness it's given
that which leads is that which has been led
   for instance: how pursuing night will want
   to dog the daylight then run out in front

TS390

the between-time, inclining towards dark
   and I am stacking wood outside
while the temperate evening is being thunderstruck
overhead the bark-like honk

   of geese again, declaring 'the turn of the tide'
   for the season of frost and the white solitude —
the world is in a bewitchment now
    as I witness the changes in the prelude

to the razzle-dazzle Fall — the evocative brew
of tree sap oozing where the saw
   severed trunk from root and limb from limb,
and the consciousness-of-moon intriguing the view

   like a torch burning in a just shut tomb
   or a planted seed conceived in a woman's womb

fog, filling the field, makes a mirage
   of the deer, browsing — day dispenses dusk —
   a drizzle drips from leaf to country dust —
insect vespers eulogize this passage
   as delicate as loving thoughts and soft
   as thistles, snowing — the smears of colors left
up on the branches make their final collage
   in Summer's bountiful decline — the freedom
   of leaf-fall is an incubated wisdom
gathering momentum   birds encourage
   my thinking with migration   in a tender
   moment   the mind prepares for the cloth-of-Winter
the matron moon applies her silver rouge —
      the hart at peace with Summer hears: *surrender*

TS370

the heron, from a meditative state,
   moved its snowy face... and like a yawn
   stretched one jointed leg out... slow...and down
(its watery image expressing a visual quote)
   and then it tucked it back into a puff
   of feathers, keeping the leg it stood on stiff —
its elegant self and driftwood perch a site
   as wondrous as any seen   in paradise
   there are many treasures at a heron's house...
even more than one can contemplate —

   I won't forget it waking up to flight
   as if more consciousness than weight
and how it flew away... to re-alight...
   somewhere else beyond what I can say

FALL

EQUINOX

TS105

forget the honeysuckle-saturated
wind... moth wing soft and full of dawn

forget how March was gently overthrown

forget the way that February had
the innocent audacity to plant
the thought of Spring in what was Winter bent

forget that the cool consistency of mud
was transubstantiated into flowers
and how the eye was blazing with their flavors

forget the scherzo of the katydid

forget the things that leave and blow away

for the blue jay sky is full of sun today
dispensing depth to all that dark has hid

for Fall has roused herself from Summer's bed

TS100

I keep on coming back to this: this road
setting me threading through the shadowy wood
   confettied by generous trees and an episode
of nomadic clouds with slanted spears of amber
sunlight pouring through their grey October
   bodies — here where the fabulous leaf and blade,
in their sweetly smelling entropy, pretend
as if their lives were coming to an end —
   where boisterous black-robed crows intrude
upon the wind's soliloquy   with tales
of man's expanses bejeweled by verdant isles
   I keep on coming back to the abode
of myth quickened in to matter
with all its threats and promises of weather

TS540

gothic clouds came in, in a swirling might
shoved by a wind as fierce as it was feral
ranging over field and forest plot
portending the possibility of peril

the trees' twiggy ends collided in a snarl
and as if getting ready for a fight
they flexed their rigid arms and made a whirl-
ing noise… like hissing in the key of fright

then, dramatically the grey drape
pulled apart… and a flash flood light
(that waited like a caged thing to escape)
discharged a brilliance with the speed of thought

stunning the eye and leaving the mouth agape
before the thunder could fire a single shot

TS90

if conspiracy it was then all
   of that is in the open   now   among
   the old leaves are the changing ones — the sting
of frost is rumored to have stunned the will

   of gardens in the lowlands — burdock bristles
with burrs that once were in a flower thrall
and a sense of insect urgency spill-
   s through the meadow (scratchy-like, it rustles)

when the winds come all pell mell,
   cluttering earth with the leavy red dead —
   here is an intrigue binding as honor and blood
borne in the body of triumphant Fall

   Autumn's inhale heralds Summer's exile

the chipmunk hides its harvest in the wall

TS117

a (waiting-for-Winter) woodpile wanted stack-
ing   instead of staying a chaos of levels and slants
its very nature called to be unstuck
and ordered   in the way Emotion haunts
itself for an untangled language   I tugged and pick-
ed and pulled the would-be-fire from its jumble
and reassembled it to interlock
like puzzle pieces — I felt fleet and nimble
with my wits which, working with my wants,
created something at a different angle —
what was once a muddle of intents
became a clear cut stack of wood of simple
elegance that satisfied my sense
of solidness as well as sense for symbol

TS248

after the quick cold came and left
the blue experience of frost, a shift
took place and Indian Summer happened at last
giving my melancholy mind a lift

    (like the way it was when, from Winter's crust,
    sprouts stretched out like fingers from a fist —
    when the wind's harsh voice grew soft
    and the peaceable sun, through aspiring morning mist,
    lit the world like a bright idea)

my inquisitive eye was impressed with the swirling sea
of trees, undressing in the ferny wood...
inviting me to come inside to see
the season in its most flamboyant mood
before the coming Winter interlude

TS92

the green revolt that overthrew the Winter,
moons ago, is almost over   now
Autumn unthrones the impetuous Summer pretender
beheading the stems and turning the meadows to straw

imposing a standard and overthrowing the order —
and rain... a chilling reign becomes the rule —
lately, I have seen the chipmunk scamper
to its hideout, snake flow down its hole

and witnessed the fleshy thud and juicy dismember-
ment of apples fallen on the field — a vast
'conveying hence' has happened: the monarch butter-
fly has flown these Berkshire hills in quest

of safer places — *Fall is come* I whisper
adapt I hear *or else adopt disaster*

TS416

an eight-point buck was shot to death today
(a lesser presence in the woods this May)
  with all the ways to execute a plan
it didn't have to happen quite this way

  when death has to happen then let it be neat as a pin
  but here was one with an extra violent spin:
he shot the buck… but still it got away
  and hence the bloody chase and closing in

could ever a motion, an image or language convey
the shock of being in a bullet's way
  the red pulse growing thin
the final shooting in the place it lay

  there's just no telling what possesses a man
  and that of course is how the poem began

TS401

time was up — the maple dropped its yellow
glitter on the coffee colored field
finally   all clinging has to yield
   if there is to be something fresh to follow

even dying will get over-old
   and, as with Winter, weary of itself
   for being mired in a greenless gulf
and sets itself to come in from the cold

   the wind whose intent was to take the leaf
informed me with a worry when it rose...
though some place deeper than my thinking knows
   that giving purchase to a negative belief

will provide a foothold where misfortune grows
and like a barren tree have no relief

TS408

you may remember how the last scene ended?
the life of the autumny leaves had been extended
    as far as what good sense allowed... and by
the millions, on the back of the wind, descended

    'til their once green faces against the glittering sky
    became an imprint on the mental eye —
the drama was, as usual, quite splendid
    even if the Summer had to die

you may remember how the weather tended
by degrees to become more frozen-minded
    when a few last restless geese broadcast their cry
across the dimming evening before they were blended

    like ghosts in the grey dark that was now the sky
like a mind whose sense of self had been expanded

TS124

my mind is a room to contemplate forever
a book of being from a cosmic shelf
to tell a tale that tells about my self —
there my thoughts can turn into a river
of air to hasten Autumn off the tree
by simply blowing wind-thoughts thought by me —
I can make the moon a waning sliver
or emboss the black above with the marvelous flare
of stars forcing my eyes to lift and stare
while through transfigured woods the sinuus silver
mist is slithering over its frosty floor
I can imagine remaining or making a door —
Winter's coming — I can think it over
and love whatever it is I will discover

TS270

leaving is always the choice to which Autumn is led:
the air a drizzle and dropped to inclement degrees
as geese, in a fanfare and dirge, wedge their vees
toward other climes where they may safely bed —
a too tight nest can birth a grief
or force one to a more enlarged belief
of what home is   when wing and wind are wed
the choices are: to deny the need to fly
or take the risk and jump into the sky
who wouldn't choose to leave than stay instead?
the sky is a world as wide as one thinks it to be
encouraging travel as far as it takes to feel free
it happens as often as lifting up one's head
or at the grave site lowering the dead

TS93

I thought the frost would decimate the discourse
of the crickets and wipe their meadowy house
away — I thought the swaddling sun would go
withdrawing from the world's rocky body
like a mother from her breast-indulging baby
I thought the dandelion would have lost its halo
and the ripply pond made stiff as slate
with a north wind whirling down to turn it white
I thought the wood would have turned calico
and turbulent skies would pour through holes in it
I thought the world that I wondered at
was dead and done... and yet this isn't so
like a spirit, it hovers about its corporeal temple
there's more than meets the eye — it's just that simple

nightfall fell… in the gesture that a flock
of geese exhibit, when their wings fan out
like parachutes, to bring their reptile feet
down gently on the planet's grassy back…
the sight, though subtle, is a common mat-
ter: day disintegrating in to dark —
it is a pretty piece of cosmic work
this   seamlessness   so auto-magic that
the experience is floated like an ark
along my rivery nerves becalmed by it —
inevitable change has come, as Summer's hot
mentality becomes the cool remark
of Autumn…effortlessly as geese that set
as smoothly as a sky turned back to black

TS397

in the gut of the dark lay the dormant light... then dawn
and starlings swarming on stark boughs
their castenet-chirps at all-time highs —
   then emptying the trees like Fall come down
a second time, I felt a blank surprise
when all fell silent and shivery morning rose
   towards noon and all that that makes known —
always out of the chaos the quiet grows
whatever isn't now will be the news
   to come   as sure as what was at the crown
is now the color underneath my shoes
I marvel how the vegetation shies
   away from imminent November's brawn
and how the milkweed opens by my thighs

TS400

rain... rain and wind... a wind as warm
as one that blows itself through mid-September
though by my calendar it says November
   though Autumn's already leapt from the trees in a swarm
   and frost has visited, it makes one wonder
how a month so infamous could be so tender
   those expecting snow could be alarm-
ed at such an unexpected lack of temper
something like a lion with a whimper —
   I for one have found the whole thing charm-
ing like a bush whose bloom forgot to wither
or Consciousness who went a wee bit further
   than expected by the fearful or the norm —
who knows what it will be like by December

TS404

the sun was diffused to a fuzzy ball of silver
as it felt its rising way through an autumn fog
trunks of trees were penciled in and over
it like ghostly masts awaiting rig-

ging — this was the curious way the episode started
by middle morning, light ripped through the rag-
gy greyness and triumphantly escorted
the blueness in — but the trees began to tug

and twirl when a wind whirled in and asserted
its decision to rough up the stationary air —
any hope for calm by then was thwarted —
my hair was wet and thunder shocked my ear

and still the journey south was not aborted
by the feathered ones whose call was sound and clear

TS402

a phantomy fog skated across the wetlands
bullet rain dropped for long seconds
somewhere from a far distance   farmhands
culled the cows and heart shaped hoovey-ponds

were printed in the cocoa colored mud —
the trees, before the wintry wind had had
its way with them, were swimming in a flood
of November light that lit them up like blood

noisy turkeys rummaged in nearby woods
where suddenly a cluster of watery beads

were shot like arrows from a spider's thread
when grazed by one who had its feathers spread

dramatic as a breeze dispatching seeds

or force at rest transformed to speed

TS256

the story, as fresh as success and old as loss
   begins by being neatly poised between
the two – the sky becomes an opaque wash
   and under it the hemlocks lurch and moan
     while an owl makes a bough its parapet
      the mouse, at the hole of its house, is aware of it
   its smelling sweeping the midnight like a broom

   those that love the dark do not see doom
     the hungry field mouse, for example, that
     got eaten by the roving mountain cat
   the clouds pulled apart and the curious mirror moon
like a yellow eye observed the sudden hush
   of lungs and circulation that all too soon
the feelings feel and the Reason must discuss

gaunt-faced, birdsong silent
mountains and nerve-like rivers in cold descent
through bush and scrub in a ganglionic tangle:
grey in a November mood... since all
that flourished (once upon the Summer) fell
when a wind and rain came in and had a rumble
with the woods and wrestled color to its knees
(now the eye adds more to what it knows)
butterflies are fled, the zipz of bumble-
bees are far enough away to seem
like legends now the weather's present aim
is to reduce the world to a single
frozen state of mind   like Winter
these are the days that are savored by the hunter

TS122

remember why you came   remember that
you can't forget   the cardinal in his red
hot hood and cape or icy blue jay's chat-
tering   although the fickle Fall has fled
from Summer's long green arms to Winter's stark
society   with awesome acrobat
panache   the white storm's come to turn the dark
geography into a brilliance that
can make the heart, once overcast, feel heady:
the bleak beauty indelibly writing its mark
upon the mind... to make its seeing steady....
like the unmistakable sight of a sudden spark
in a blackened space that you were peering at
remember? you'll remember when you're ready

TS268

the plot is epic in proportion... like
the hungry-journey of a field mouse
   across a cornfield with each stalk a spike
and a tidal wave of snow above her house

half the time it's light out and the hawks
   are circling — the other half it's night, awake
with owls and many other sorts of shocks
   to cause the noblest of hearts to shake

   it's not as if this hasn't happened before —
the big attraction is that paradise
   has many things for field mice to explore —
practice makes the novice hunter wise

to where the seeds and berries be... and thoughts
   of something being eaten... to be sure

TS118

where the fir trees skirt the field, a single file
of turkeys put their imprints in the pale
November snow which day had freshly drop-
ped - and one who had hunger hatching in his belly
was taking quick advantage of their folly:
their scratching and dawdling...using time up —
the canine limbicly loping closer
its sense of smell incisive as a laser
reading the air like an eye can read a map —
and dusk deepening the duo-tone
of alive black stripes upon the plane
of silent white while somewhere went the sweep-
ing sound of turkey feathers brushing snow —
with the lilac sky reduced to an indigo glow

TS415

Spring: a memory and prophecy
   and I am sandwiched in between the two
   remembering one and hoping the other is true —
I could be on a drifting raft at sea:
   a dot where air and water are pressed together
   subject to the mercurial whims of weather
with alien animals over and under me —
   again and again stars freckle the black
   and over and over again the morning comes back
exposing snow   as far as I can see
   the fact of the matter is: I'm in a space
   that can be called 'The Isle of Anyplace'
and it's as good as any place can be
and that's as good as any space can be

TS409

an animal, during darkness, waded through
the meadow under a white hot snow —
its freshly minted prints cut a row
of marks from one side of my point of view,

across it, to the other… and withdrew —
what need or urge could drive a creature so…
into a world zero and below
with what or whom had it a rendezvous

and was it *going from* or *coming to*
or something other I have yet to know…
whatever it is, it occupies me though
for a mind creating metaphor can do

all sorts of hocus pocus with a doe
traversing midnight and November snow

TS119

at the south side of things the clicking drip
of liquefying snowflakes segment time —
    evening's eastward-inching shadows slip
along the snow's blue back to counsel me

to watch what three dimensions and a flame
    can do to calibrate my being here —
yet, this *wake* reality that I resume
    to live in day to day to year to year

    is born of the Quantum Universe... as sure
as the moon commits its luminescent arch
    and planet nature to the dark desire
over earth, or the Summer summoned birch

tree re-appropriates an Autumn stretch
    of lapis sky whose face is veiled by stars

TS94

before white-faced Winter hushed the woods
the lukewarm wind cast off the thistles
driven to death-defying deeds
by being willing to be launched as vessels

for the transportation of their seeds —
before the wraith-like Winter, in a blizzard,
wiped the visual world away, the weeds
were in an orgy and Autumn was all that mattered —

before Fall submerged in a bath of colors
and Summer was thriving in all of the neighborhoods
the way it is was terminal as flowers
and *what will be* an embryo, the woods

had harbored like an incubating thistle
until its inevitable span of hours

WINTER

SOLSTICE

TS289

picture this: you're looking down on you
who's standing in the middle of a meadow

the sun is overcast so casts no shadow

the meadow stretches from you to a view
of trees that form an equidistant circle

the cyclic year is in its Winter cycle
erasing the past and preparing its future, too

the trees crisscross their branches into arches
and from each one a different direction stretches

and you will turn to one and then go through

I can give you dozens of examples
of what I have encountered in my rambles
I've hair enough that's grey to say it's true
all you have to do is check my temples

TS130

Winter's pale body coaxes me
to enter ever deeper into time
  to go down through to my undermind
to make myself a temporary home

  this is the way it is at Autumn's end
  the weightless flake can be gathered by the pound
the beings with wings and the will to go are gone
  and quadrupeds put prints upon the pond

below the world's snowy overtone
the gaunt geography contracts to stone
  while the spidery wind, whenever it's around,
speaks a language starker than pantomime

  the woodchuck's snuggled under the downy mound
  synchronistic with the Winter mind

TS151

the world puts on a masque of the death of Winter
and the winds are the chorus everywhere they wander
the woods shiver whenever it feels them come…
ferocious sometimes — reminding them to remember

that the dying isn't close to being done
there're snowstorms still to measure by the ton —
inhibitor of feather, foot and fin
and presently bold enough to defy the sun

the underworld's waiting to begin
to push its meaning through the earth again
I make my memory remember   that
the Summer loves this place I'm standing in

though Summer be living only in my thought
but here's where there's a miracle in the plot

TS135

the cold virility of time turns water
to ice and makes mandalas out of rain
the far from Summer meadow is a ruin
   below four feet of fallen Winter

a corpulent moon delineates a vein
   of branches rivering the nocturnal air
   and reiterates their bony shadows near
a quick cloud causes a temporary stain

   I looked on this from a window in a door
one middle-of-the-night   between two sleeps
I keep reinventing their relationships
   kinds that cause my curious mind to stir

somewhere a she-coyote feeds her pups
   somewhere else a fawn has lost its mother

TS431

it's not escaped me how the north wind drove
the geese away, and how the rain, wave
   after wave, scuttled the leaves one blustery
afternoon — it's not escaped me that
the light grows more anemic, rut
   and puddle thicken, and all about's turned wintry
that feed is scarce for hooved and feathered things
and a singeing ice-like air arrests my lungs
   that the covert mice come in to rob the pantry
that time is thief enough to steal my face
and leave grey hairs and wrinkles in its place
   it's not escaped me that a former bounty
like an affluent idea redefined
works in the soil that rests in my future mind

TS449

there're some of us who live at the edge of things
different as a desert to a sea
out there the wind does mischief if it sings
but that's the consequence when one is free

Summer succumbs to Winter's icy fangs
the reign of snow gets overthrown by fire
and you can't mistake the thunder as it bangs
at heaven's ceiling with a hero's ire

it's here one's thinking rightfully belongs
though tongues may differ the tale's the same
repeated in mythologies and songs
to civilize but not to make too tame

as natural as fresh air to new lungs
and logical as calculated sums

TS271

were I a hungry hunter with just a sling
and trusted my hand to hurl a stone with it...
if I had the presence of mind and skill to hit
two birds with one stone... I'd sing
and dance around my fire during dark
to thank the watchful beings for the spark
of the Supernatural illuminating
me... my thanks assuring me the chance
that I will do another harvest dance
(the present comes from one's imagining)
it doesn't take a prophet or a sage
to prove that   fortune comes   at any age
the wish and the wish's fulfillment is the thing
like freeing two birds from one cage

calm (the heart of the hurricane) the eye:
central to the storm's cosmology
with the blurry material world swirling by
its catastrophic noise desiring me

like the amniotic cave through which I came
and the curving world of astrology
circling the embryonic Earth   I am
enwombed by time and its biology

inseparable as light around a flame
unknown to dogma and theology:
the virile seed in the dark damp loam...
safe, even in a hurricane

that stirs desire and psychology
as if intending to off-center me

TS144

on and on and on and on and on
   the sibyllant North comes slithering underneath
   my door like syllables sswhistling between the teeth
pushing the room's warm air like a broom

   there's something magical about the sound
   that has the strength to push a man around

sometimes it shows its Self by spinning in
   an aggregate of snow and shards of ice
   at others it's an invisible wedge through space
pushing and pulling whatever it passes upon

   I'm always amazed whenever the branches respond
   with the perfect pitch, as if from a Merlin's wand…
their angled arms with the banshee air between —
   the wind is like this sometimes in my dreams

TS131

the full-bellied moon lit like a lantern
insistently ascends in an indigo space
as the clickity-clacking branches again return
and press dark moving veins across her face

while the uterine sky in its dark exalted fate
with stars (like children choosing to be born)
imprints my witnessing Consciousness like slate
is printed with the presence of a fern

and I, enchanted, determine how remote
or close exists the place of paradise

everywhere I look is a Wintry site:
the flowerless meadow widowed by blizzards and ice
while the calligraphy of branches branching quote
themselves in shadow from a Cosmic note

TS137

out of the stuff of stars our bodies come

who wouldn't want you just the way you are

I can feel your physical female flame
as if the male I am borrowed your name

you are softer than the moss that Nature
put between two birch trees in the woods
as lovely as a flower-puddled pasture
the memory remembers in the future

being human beings, my heart bleeds
the same as yours and wants your opposite
anatomy as a flood plain welcomes floods

you hold me as a hero holds his deeds

we are inseparable as snow is white
with the salient stuff of stars in the Room-of-the-night

TS133

like the pulse and impulse of blood through its circular flume
and ceaseless revolutions of the globe
time goes on — the quartet seasons strobe —
and now the white transfiguration's come
the wind-rattled woods roar and thunder
driving the plants and animals under
making the worlds of sky and earth the same
blank swirling picture — its limbic essence
demanding I take notice of its presence
shutting the world down like a corpse in a tomb —
but afterwards when all the storming's done
when the eye is bedazzled by snow under sun
Time has turned the Earth some more, and me
who stirs like an egg asleep deep in a bird

TS138

Winter's hiatus… and Spring's tentative tease
melting the world by dramatic degrees —
morning steaming with white evaporation
and icicles, like jingling keys, letting loose

their slippery grips for a watery destination —
meanwhile with an excited wagging motion
from a rush of wind and rain the woods awake
predicting the season's transubstantiation

to grassy green spear from feathery flake —
the whole affair, so mythological-like,
bubbles from under the unconscious mind
breaching my thoughts like a flood through a dike

more vast than anyone could apprehend
to reinvent what's coming to an end

TS285

a wraith-like fog spilled out of the woods, slither-
ing into a field where it coiled itself together —
had the Reaper arrived   at last   was Winter dead

the pond, too... smoldered and steamed, shaggy
strands of mist glided over its body

the horizon became a jagged yellow thread
that burst into a fireball, torching
night, wiping away the over-arching
stars and all the other dark things overhead

Change had triumphed again, even if
Winter didn't die, even if
the idea of Spring had only rolled over in bed
just slightly awakened before being pulled back to sleep
the fog retreating   again the snow piling deep

TS132

the cold that metamorphosed rain to lace
descended   in the medium of space

the meadow's floor rose up a couple of feet
as white as the sky it aspired to   with the lean
grey woods disintegrating   in between

I remember   the earth (in a lover's heat)
with her flurry of seeds unfurling into sonic
air and the buds inspired to a manic
resonance lovely as they were sweet

and all this bounty as far as I can see
was mine for the seeing   if only inside of me
this Summer-equivalent meadow full of beat-
ing insect wings and sounds of every flavor
now metamorphosed into snow behavior

TS290

this is not the first time this has happened:
I'm standing in the middle of an opened
space, which is encircled by the stark
asymmetry of trees — in this meadow
with me is Winter — across the pearl snow
my footprints make a linear remark
from where I am to where I chose to enter
like a radius from perimeter to center —
I can reconsider going back
the way I came or take a new route in —
regardless, I must enter the woods again —
there're countless doorways through the trees to pick —
whatever it is I'll find I'll have to face —
it's not the last time I will leave a space

TS143

I see what Winter does — I watch the way
grey smudges expropriate the sky
   how the white sheet earth is scribbled with
the autographs of rabbit, deer and turkey

how the still woods drip with a foggy broth —
the weather's new philosophy is forth
   and back and forth again... the cold clench
of ice loosens and smashes itself to death

rivulets gather together to circle the hunch
of a hill — a pond appears — and yet the staunch
   and cyclic Consciousness of night comes in
turning my breaths to ghosts, putting the crunch

   back in the snow, and reddening up my skin
   though rivulets will snake the hill again

when, I wondered, would the final stroke
of Winter come and in its inevitable wake
when would the presence of flower and flowering weed
arrive — when a ruckus of geese declared that soon
the trill of peepers would be heard beneath the moon —
then a stormy lid of clouds began to shred
and let the blue above pour in like water
dousing every thawing thing with glitter —
then the clouds closed in – yet the mood
of waking heaved at the root and tip of the twig:
that desire and drive for small things to grow big
even after Winter's careless tread
the tentative bulbs were pushing through
and the air had a temperate temper to it too

TS176

winter's inevitable charge to liquefy
   made earth a mess of muddy puddles
   the low-arced sun was building up its muscles
making it warm if anything wanted to fly

   tufts of straw stuck up like hair on knuckles
from island-like mounds surrounded by ebbing snow
immense accomplishments from small things grow:
   a river, remember, was once a crisscross of trickles

some canny mammal with a cushy paw
   scrawled a message in a dotted line
   on what was left of the bone-white time
it's true, I was intrigued enough to follow

   but let it be as I was, left alone,
and driven by an impulse of my own

TS428

before the horizontal beam, before
it seeped between the great black hem
of night and the world's distant eastern rim
like a crack of light from underneath a door

before the hand-like silhouette the limb
put out to hold a tiny bulging planet
which only briefly rested on it

before February's zodiac grew dim
against the sky until it melted in it
like the present tense into the past

before the delicate imperceptible crust
of snow had sunrise-pink convening on it
and night grew insubstantial as a ghost

all of this was very very dark

TS136

would it matter if I named the country where
  the cold is serpent-coiled about the house
  keeping away the squirrel and rabbit and grouse
where the weather wanders in with its white desire
  spilling over everything that sleeps
  (desire is a thing that plays for keeps
however vague the nature of its future)
  where icicle fangs hang over the eves as big
  around as my thigh and longer than my leg
growing by melting and melting until they expire
  some of them are delicate as bird bones
  and self destruct with bell-like overtones
as if it were the swan song of a creature
in ecstasy over its phoenix nature

TS302

I awoke about a week ago
   aware of morning mixed with robin speeches
   to prove reality is made with wishes
I heard the red winged blackbirds, too
   sounding earlier than I remember
   but then again, so did December —
just like the hand of death, you never know
   exactly when the greening time will want
   to make itself once more be relevant,
the birds declared (as if I never knew)
   they were the death rattle in Winter's voice
   despite how it might re-invent the ice
again   they sang, *believe it, Winter's through*
   which seems to me to be quite sound advice

I've been here many times before:
the woods, loud with February wind
and snow hurrying itself into a pond
   and as if someone slightly jarred a door
to let a shaft of light into the room
(that up 'til now had sanctuaried gloom)
   the sun comes calling from behind a cloud, pour-
ing over reasons I should come and play
the main one being that he cannot stay
   for Winter isn't over yet for sure
but like its former self, alias Autumn,
it is ephemeral as the rising phantom
   mist that slinked along the forest's floor
shrouding the quiet body of the blossom

TS177

after Summer's leaf proliferation
turned into a mass defoliation
Winter's gentle killing came in in-
crements of frost and snowy inches

by then the air had thinned of finches
and other such fair-weather creatures, sun
addicted with the wherewithal to go
a blizzard brewed and made a blank scenario
of the meadow like a paper wanting writing on

and under it, in suspended animation,
were those awaiting the year's next incarnation
when the meadow is layered with weeds and flowers again
sunward rising like columns to a temple
in honor of Spring whose killing is as gentle

TS446

this schizophrenic weather, this will pass
  the crimson innuendo on the limb
  the unfurling urge of a crocus (like a thumb
from a fist of fingers) in the not-yet-grass

  and animals from the subterranean womb
assessing the woods with their sensitive noses
and the not-since-last-year blackbird noises
  convening on branches, trumpeting Spring from its tomb

the thinning winds' icy voices
  the blue fractal frost undone on the glass
  the delirium of clouds falling, this will pass
all the inertia bridging itself to a crisis

  to inflict a wound and salve the wound's distress
to hold a bouquet one must make a fist

TS432

fog smoldering like fire in the wood
the late snows risen to their flooding speed
and the report of lilies in the neighborhood
is presently potential being freed

innocent hope again is still alive:
sprouting out of the mud to the blue above
like a serpent slipping out of its papery sleeve
or a principle you just learned to believe

this is the way that natural things behave
going in or coming from the grave

that impulse of a transcendental mood
expressing itself in a psycho-sensual deed

that stronger-than-dying impulse to arrive

that I have witnessed even in a weed

TS165

the indiscriminate fog that moped around
for days had lifted — then a helter-skelter wind
rumpled the clouds and pruned the branches that
had semi-urgent business with the ground

while Winter melted and made mud out of it
I could feel the trees wishing the weather would let
them leave Winter and make that delicious sound
they make… and thinking that, the sun came out

like a lucid thought in a schizophrenic mind
the shadowy stripes of trunks along the land
made myriad sundials showing the season was set-
ing as a wedge of throaty geese, northern bound,

brought back that sound that said it was time to depart
but switched it to say that now it is time to start

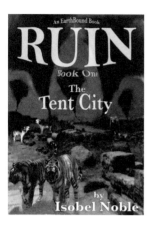

ORDER FORM

RUIN: Book One: The Tent City $16.66 ea.
No. of copies_____ Total enclosed $_____

RUIN: Book Two: The City of Life $25.00 ea.
No. of copies_____ Total enclosed $_____

Temple Sonnets $12.00 ea.
No. of copies_____ Total enclosed $_____

Elephants of the Tsunami $ 9.99 ea.
No. of copies_____ Total enclosed $_____

**Send to: EARTHBOUND BOOKS   **Check or Money Order Only
             P.O. Box 549
             North Egremont, MA 01252

ame _____ Telephone No. _____

reet _____ Apartment No. _____

ty, State, Zip _____, _____, _____